FUNDAMENTAL PHYSICS

Electricity and Magnetism

GERARD CHESHIRE

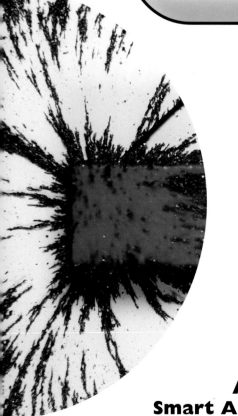

A⁺
Smart Apple Media

First published in 2006 by Evans Brothers Ltd
2A Portman Mansions,Chiltern Street,
London W1U 6NR

This edition published under license from
Evans Brothers Ltd. All rights reserved.
Copyright © 2006 Evans Brothers Ltd.

Series editor: Harriet Brown, Editor: Harriet
Brown, Design: Robert Walster, Illustrations:
Q2A Creative

Published in the United States by
Smart Apple Media
2140 Howard Drive West, North Mankato,
Minnesota 56003

U.S. publication copyright © 2007
Smart Apple Media
International copyright reserved in all
countries. No part of this book may be
reproduced in any form without written
permission from the publisher.
Printed in China

Library of Congress Cataloging-in-
Publication Data

Cheshire, Gerard, 1965-
Electricity and magnetism / by Gerard Cheshire.
p. cm. — (Fundamental physics)
Includes index.
ISBN-13: 978-1-58340-994-7
1. Electricity—Juvenile literature.
2. Magnetism—Juvenile literature. I. Title.

QC527.2.C53 2006
537—dc22   2006042240

9 8 7 6 5 4 3 2 1

Contents

Introduction

Electricity and magnetism are an important part of life in many parts of the world. You are likely to use electricity every day, without even thinking

about it. When you switch on a television, ring a doorbell, or travel in a car, electricity and magnetism are involved.

This book takes you on a journey to discover what electricity is, how it is produced, and how we have come to rely on it. Find out how magnets work, discover some unusual places in which they are found, and learn about how electricity and magnetism are related. Learn about famous scientists who uncovered the secrets of electricity and magnetism many years ago, and take a journey into the future to find out how advances in microchip technology may change our world.

This book also contains feature boxes that will help you unravel more about the mysteries of electricity and magnetism. Test yourself on what you have learned so far, investigate some of the concepts discussed, find out more key facts, discover some of the scientific findings of the past, and see how these might be utilized in the future.

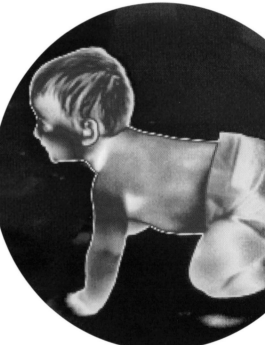

DID YOU KNOW?

▶ Look for these boxes—they contain surprising and fascinating facts about electricity and magnetism.

TEST YOURSELF

▶ Use these boxes to see how much you've learned. Try to answer the questions without looking at the book, but take a look if you are really stuck.

INVESTIGATE

▶ These boxes contain experiments you can carry out at home. The equipment you will need is usually cheap and easy to find.

TIME TRAVEL

These boxes contain scientific discoveries from the past and fascinating developments that pave the way for the advance of science in the future.

ANSWERS

At the end of this book, on pages 46 and 47, you will find the answers to questions from the "Test yourself" and "Investigate" boxes.

GLOSSARY

Words highlighted in **bold** are described in detail in the glossary on pages 46 and 47.

What is electricity?

Electricity has been part of our lives since prehistoric times, so it would be misleading to say that anyone had actually discovered it. Ancient man witnessed electricity in the form of lightning every time there was a thunderstorm. Some people viewed electricity as a powerful message from the gods, but today, electricity is more fully understood. We use electricity hundreds of times every day—whenever we flick a light switch, turn on the television, or use a telephone.

◀ Electricity dominates many parts of the world. Life without electricity would be almost unrecognizable to many of us.

MAGICAL ATTRACTION

In ancient Greece around 2,300 years ago, scientists—known then as "natural philosophers"—noticed things in nature that taught them about electricity. They experimented with amber, a fossilized tree resin, which is used today to make jewelry. When scientists rubbed amber and fur together, they found that the amber acquired a mysterious and "magical" ability to attract lightweight objects, such as feathers.

The ancient Greeks did not know what was causing the amber to behave in this way, but their name for amber (elektron) was used as the basis of the word "electric." Today, we know that amber acquires this power of attraction when it becomes charged with electricity, or has an "electric charge."

DID YOU KNOW?

▶ It is estimated that some electrical storms create enough electricity to power the entire United States for 20 minutes.
▶ At any one time, there are about 2,000 electrical storms going on in the world.

UNDERSTANDING ELECTRIC CHARGE

There are two types of electric charge, which are known as positive (+) and negative (−). Electric charges are called "positive" and "negative" because they attract each other, much like the north and south poles of a magnet (see pages 22–27). To understand how an object can become charged, it is important to know a little about atoms.

Everything in the universe—every plant and animal, every building, every planet—is made of tiny particles called atoms. At the center of each atom is a nucleus. If an atom was magnified until it was the size of a football stadium, the nucleus would be the size of a grape. The nucleus is made from even smaller particles called protons and neutrons. Protons carry a positive electric charge, and neutrons have no electric charge. The neutrons prevent the protons from repelling each other and flying apart.

A cloud of electrons surrounds the nucleus. Electrons carry a negative electric charge and balance the positive charge of the protons.

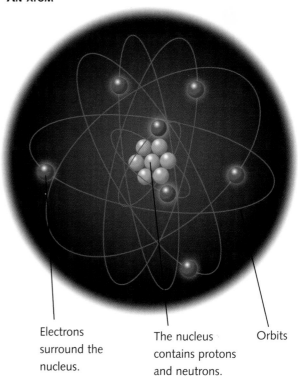

Electrons surround the nucleus.

The nucleus contains protons and neutrons.

Orbits

Overall, atoms have a "neutral" charge. When electrons move from one place to another, they carry their negative electric charge with them. The movement of electric charge, or electrons, is electricity.

ELECTRON MOVEMENT

The movement of electrons is also called an **electric current**, or **current electricity**. Some materials allow electrons to move freely—these are called "**conductors**" and include most metals. Other materials make it difficult for electrons to move—these materials are called "**insulators**" and include rubber, plastic, and amber.

◄ Amber is fossilized tree resin. Most of the world's amber is between 30 and 90 million years old. Amber is an insulator that can gain an electric charge.

STATIC ELECTRICITY

Electrons can gather on the surface of insulators. This is known as **electrostatic charge**, or **static electricity**. Objects that gain electrons become negatively charged, and those that lose electrons become positively charged. When you rub different materials together, you literally rub electrons off of one material and onto another.

When the ancient Greeks rubbed amber with a piece of fur, they rubbed negatively charged electrons off of the fur and onto the amber. The amber ended up with extra electrons sitting on its surface and therefore gained a negative electric charge. Like charges repel each other, so when the amber was held near a feather, it pushed away the feather's electrons. The feather became positively charged and was attracted to the amber.

▶ The negatively charged balloon attracts the cat's fur.

INVESTIGATE

▶ Positively or negatively charged objects try to lose their charge to become neutrally charged. To see this for yourself, inflate a balloon and rub it on a wool sweater. Next, "stick" the balloon to a wall. Notice how the balloon stays on the wall for several seconds before it falls off. Why does this happen?

By rubbing the balloon on a wool sweater, you are moving negatively charged electrons from the sweater to the balloon. The balloon becomes negatively charged with static electricity, repels electrons in the wall, and is then attracted to the resulting positive

charge of the wall. This attraction holds the two objects in contact. Eventually, the balloon's extra electrons move to the wall, and both objects become neutrally charged. With no attraction present, the balloon falls to the ground.

The next part of the experiment should be done in a dark room. Rub the balloon on a sweater again and then touch the balloon to the side of a fluorescent light bulb tube. The light bulb should glow as the electrons pass through it. This may take several attempts, but keep trying.

LIGHTNING—FEROCIOUS ELECTRICITY

A lightning bolt is hotter than the surface of the sun and is a spectacular example of static electricity in nature. During a thunderstorm, droplets of moisture in a storm cloud collide with one another. This creates an area of negative charge at the bottom of the storm cloud, which repels electrons on the ground. This makes the ground positively charged, and a strong attraction forms between the clouds and the ground. As the charges build up and the attraction grows stronger, the cloud suddenly releases its charge, which travels to the ground in the form of lightning. Be careful not to stand in an exposed area during a thunderstorm; lightning can kill.

The noise of thunder is caused by shock waves as the lightning superheats and expands the air around it. You always hear thunder after you see lightning because thunder travels at the speed of sound, 985 feet (300 m) per second, whereas the flash of lightning travels at the speed of light, an incredible 186,400 miles (300,000 km) per second.

▲ Lightning is caused by a buildup of static electricity in the atmosphere.

SHOCKING ELECTRICITY

We experience mini lightning bolts in everyday life. Sometimes you build up excess electrons on your body without realizing it. For example, if you wear rubber-soled shoes (an insulator), you can pick up electrons from carpets as you walk along. The electrons on your shoe soles repel each other and spread all over your body from your feet upward. However, they cannot escape back to the ground, as the rubber is an insulator. The electrons remain on your body until you touch an object such as a metal doorknob. The excess electrons on your hand are attracted to the metal because it becomes positively charged as its electrons are repelled. Your electrons "leap" toward the doorknob. This actually produces a small electric current and is why we feel a tiny "electric shock" in the form of a spark.

STATIC ELECTRICITY IN ACTION

Some air purifiers have filters that are charged with static electricity. The negatively charged filter is used to attract positively charged dust. These air purifiers are particularly useful for attracting minute dust particles that are too small to be picked up by traditional filters. It also means that the dust doesn't block holes, as it does in normal filters.

Photocopiers use static electricity to attract toner particles to pieces of paper so that an exact copy can be made.

If a CD becomes negatively charged with static electricity, it can attract unwanted dust. Antistatic guns are used to neutralize static electricity by firing positively charged particles at the CD and stealing back the extra electrons. The result is a neutrally charged CD that no longer attracts dust.

As clothes rub together in a dryer, they acquire an electrostatic charge. Notice the way the clothes either stick together or push away from each other when you take them out.

Batteries

Batteries are a portable, cheap, and convenient way to produce electricity. They come in all shapes and sizes, from the tiny, round batteries used to power watches to the large, heavy batteries found in cars and other vehicles. The official name for a battery is an "**electric cell**." Two or more cells joined together are known as a battery of cells. All electric cells work in the same way—they store chemical energy and change it into electrical energy.

ELECTRICITY FROM CHEMICALS

An electric cell is a can full of chemicals that produces electrons. An electric cell has two terminals. One is marked positive (+) and the other negative (−). When a copper wire is connected between the two terminals to form a **circuit** (see pages 12–17), electrons are produced at the negative terminal. The electric current flows around the completed circuit from the negative to the positive terminal. It carries electrical energy from the electric cell to wherever it is needed, to power devices such as remote controls, radios, and game consoles.

▼ Car batteries provide a car with enough electrical energy to start the engine.

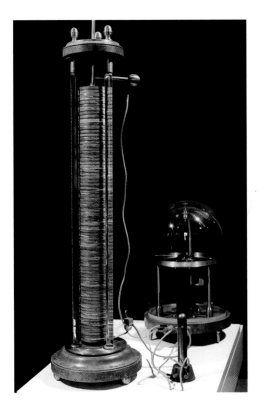

▲ The voltaic pile was the world's first electric cell.

BATTERY DISCOVERY

The first electric cell was invented by Alessandro Volta in 1800. His invention, the voltaic pile, is a stack of alternating layers of copper, cloth soaked in salt water, and zinc. This pattern repeats until the pile is around 12 inches (30 cm) tall. The positive terminal is the copper disk at the bottom, and the negative terminal is the zinc disk at the top. The reaction between the different materials generates electrons at the negative terminal. When a copper wire is attached to each end of the pile, it creates a circuit, and an electric current flows (see pages 12–17).

Fuel cells could be the electric cells of the future. They generate electricity using hydrogen and oxygen, and they create very little pollution. Unlike today's electric cells, fuel cells do not die as long as they are fed their fuel source. In the future, we may see fuel cells powering all sorts of machines, from cars to vending machines, and vacuum cleaners to cell phones.

INVESTIGATE

▶ Fruits and vegetables can be made into electric cells in a simple and safe experiment.
You will need:
Two plastic-coated copper wires with alligator clips on each end, two pieces of metal (a copper coin and a zinc nail are best), and a lemon or a potato.
(1) Push the pieces of metal into the lemon or potato. Make sure that they are not touching.
(2) Clip one wire to each piece of metal.
(3) Take the other end of each wire and place them on your tongue.

Can you feel a slight tingle? Electricity is generated by the reaction between the lemon (or potato) and the pieces of metal. The electricity travels from the lemon, along the first wire, across your tongue, and back down the other wire to the lemon.

You feel the electricity as a tingle. If you link several batteries together, the current may be large enough to light a small diode (light).

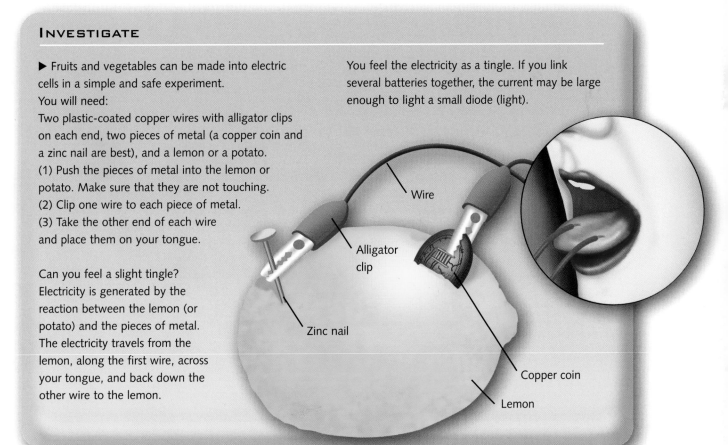

Wire

Alligator clip

Zinc nail

Copper coin

Lemon

Electric circuits

An electric current needs two things to make it flow. It must be pushed along by a source of electricity, such as an electric cell, and it needs a path along which to flow. The path is known as an electric circuit. To understand electric circuits, we need to look more closely at electric currents, how they flow, and how they are measured.

HOW ELECTRICITY FLOWS

Electricity travels almost instantly through a circuit. You have probably noticed that light comes on immediately when you flick a switch. But how does it work?

The wires of a typical circuit are made of copper metal. Copper allows electrons to travel through it—it is a conductor. When an electricity supply is connected to a circuit, electrons leave the negative terminal and immediately crash into and dislodge the electrons already in the copper wire. The free electrons in the circuit move along to make room for the new electrons, much like balls moving one another along

inside a tube. The electrons actually move very slowly individually, but the electric current is created by the chain of electrons all shifting along the circuit at the same time.

Electricity flows only when a circuit is complete and can run unbroken all the way from the negative terminal to the positive terminal of the electricity supply. If the circuit is broken, the electric current stops flowing. Switches work on this principle. In the "on" position, the circuit is complete, and the electric current flows. When the switch is pressed to the "off" position, the circuit is broken, and the current stops.

Metal atom   Cloud of electrons   Flow of electrons to positive terminal ➞

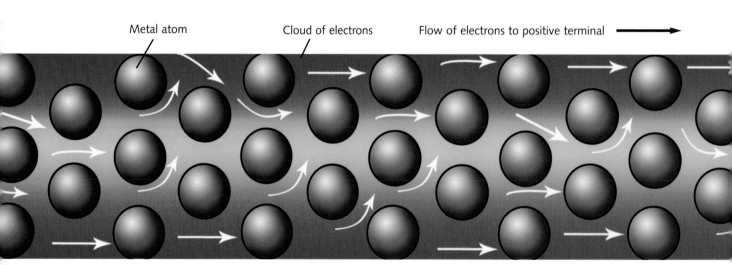

▲ This diagram shows a cross section of a wire. The cloud of electrons moves away from the negative terminal and toward the positive terminal of the electricity supply.

SERIES CIRCUITS

There are two basic ways in which a circuit can be arranged—in series and in parallel. A series circuit has only one path for the electric current to follow. The current travels from the electricity supply, through one or more components, such as a light bulb, and back to the electricity supply. In a series circuit, the components are in a row, one after the other.

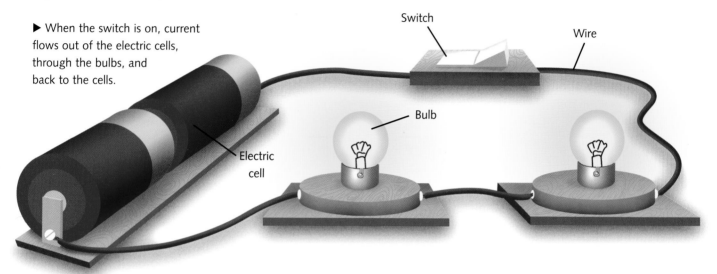

► When the switch is on, current flows out of the electric cells, through the bulbs, and back to the cells.

Switch

Wire

Bulb

Electric cell

PARALLEL CIRCUITS

A parallel circuit has two or more paths along which the electric current can travel. For example, in a parallel circuit with two light bulbs, each bulb can be on a different part of the circuit. If each part of the circuit is the same, the electric current divides equally. Parallel circuits are useful when we need to have some parts switched on and other parts switched off, such as when lighting one room in a house.

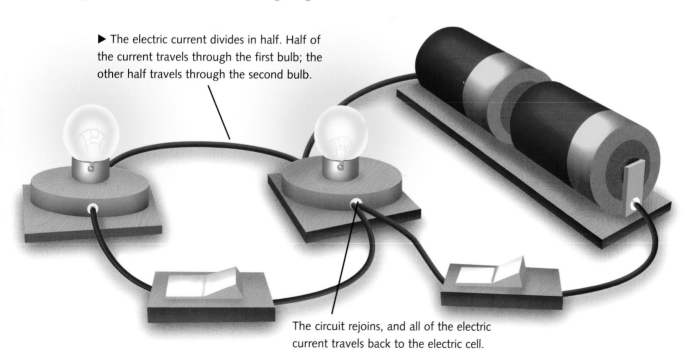

► The electric current divides in half. Half of the current travels through the first bulb; the other half travels through the second bulb.

The circuit rejoins, and all of the electric current travels back to the electric cell.

RESISTANCE AND FUSES

Components in a circuit make it harder for an electric current to flow. One light bulb connected in a series circuit would glow brightly, two light bulbs would be dimmer, and three dimmer still. The more light bulbs there are, the harder it is for the current to flow because there is more "**resistance**" in the circuit. Most components provide some resistance. The more a component resists the flow of electrons, the lower the current.

Water acts in a similar way when traveling through a hose. If the hose is wide, water can flow freely, and a large amount can pass through. If you stand on the hose, it is narrowed, and the flow slows down. The walls of the hose provide resistance in the same way as components in a circuit.

The filament of a light bulb is made from the metal tungsten and deliberately causes resistance. It slows down the electrons, which heat the filament and make it glow brightly. **Fuses** work in the same way, except that they are designed to melt when they get too hot. By doing so, they provide the weakest point in a circuit, which stops other parts of the circuit from being damaged if the current becomes too great. Fuses protect our homes from fires caused by electrical faults.

▲ The filament of a light bulb glows white-hot when electricity passes through it.

DID YOU KNOW?

▶ Graphite bombs, also known as blackout bombs, are detonated over an enemy's electrical power plants in times of war. They release clouds of ultra-fine graphite particles, and because graphite is a good conductor, the particles cause short circuits and massive disruption to a nation's electricity supply. In 1999, NATO used graphite bombs to take out 70 percent of Serbia's power supply.

KNOW YOUR SYMBOLS

The following symbols are used to represent components of a circuit. They are internationally recognized so that speakers of different languages can understand a diagram wherever they are in the world.

Bulb

Switch

Ammeter

Bulb

Resistor

Voltmeter

Electric cell

Battery (multicell)

Wire

Motor

Buzzer

SHORT CIRCUITS

Electricity always takes the path of least resistance. If wires in a circuit are not insulated and touch each other, the electric current takes the quickest route to the positive terminal of the electricity supply. This prevents the circuit from working properly and is called a "**short circuit.**" Old cables with worn coverings are dangerous because they can easily create short circuits. Another frequent cause of short circuits is the presence of water. Water is a good conductor of electricity and is able to find its way into the smallest of places to make annoying and unwanted electrical connections.

▼ Short circuits can have devastating consequences. Sparks from a short circuit blew up this oil tanker.

MEASURING CURRENT

Electric current is measured in amperes, or amps (A). One amp is about one million billion electrons per second flowing around the circuit. Electric current is not "used up" by components in a circuit. This means that exactly the same number of electrons enter and leave each component. An ammeter is a device that is used to measure the size of the current. In a series

▶ In a series circuit, electric current is the same at all points of the circuit. Both of these ammeters would show the same reading.

MEASURING CURRENT IN A SERIES CIRCUIT

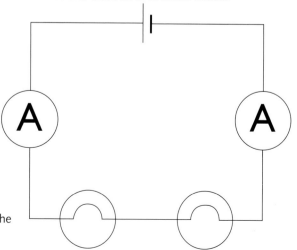

circuit, the current is the same at all points of the circuit. In a parallel circuit, the current varies depending on how many loops there are within the circuit. This is because the current is divided between the loops.

▶ In a parallel circuit, the current divides equally if the resistance of each loop is the same. Ammeters 1 and 2 would each show the total current. Ammeters 3 and 4 would each show half of the total current.

WHAT IS VOLTAGE?

Voltage is a measure of how hard an electricity supply pushes an electric current around a circuit. The bigger the voltage, the bigger the push, and the bigger the current. Batteries usually have a voltage of between 3 and 12 volts (V). The electric supply to your home is around 120 V.

MEASURING VOLTAGE IN A PARALLEL CIRCUIT

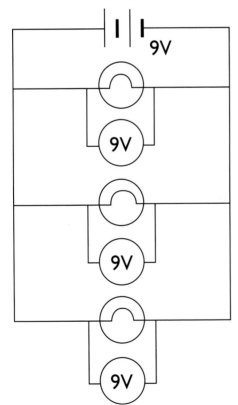

▲ In a parallel circuit, the voltage across each component represents the entire supply voltage of the battery.

MEASURING VOLTAGE

An electric current carries electrical energy, also known as electrical potential energy, which powers components in a circuit. As the current travels around a circuit, its electrical potential energy is used up by the components. When the current returns to the electric cell at the end of the circuit, it has less energy than it had at the start.

The difference between the energy at the start of the circuit and at the end is called the **potential difference**. Potential difference is another name for voltage. To measure voltage, we use a voltmeter to measure the difference between the energy entering a component or electric cell and the energy leaving it.

MEASURING VOLTAGE IN A SERIES CIRCUIT

▶ In a series circuit, the voltage across each component can be added together to give the entire supply voltage of the battery.

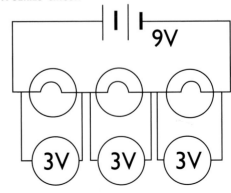

The units used to describe electricity come from the names of scientists who made valuable contributions to our understanding of electricity.

What?	Who?		Why?
The volt (V)—the unit for voltage, or potential difference.	Italian scientist Alessandro Giuseppe Antonio Volta (1745–1827)		He invented the world's first battery, the voltaic pile. The important electrical unit, the volt, was named in his honor in 1881.
The ampere (A)—the unit for electric current. One amp is about one million billion electrons per second.	French scientist Andre-Marie Ampere (1775–1836)		He established the relationship between electricity and magnetism and developed the science of electromagnetism (see pages 28–34). The ampere was named in his honor in 1881.
The ohm (Ω)—the unit of electrical resistance.	German scientist Georg Simon Ohm (1789–1854)		He developed Ohm's Law, which states that in a circuit, the voltage, or potential difference, and the current are related.

TEST YOURSELF

▶ Draw and name all 11 electrical symbols.
▶ Draw a series circuit and a parallel circuit. Show where you would place the ammeters and voltmeters to measure the electric current and voltage in each circuit.

4

National grids to microchips

Electric circuits come in all shapes and sizes. Enormous electric circuits span hundreds of miles and supply thousands of homes with electricity. These large-scale circuits are called macrocircuits, from the Greek word "makros," which means "large." Medium-sized circuits, called mesocircuits, supply electricity within homes, offices, and schools. Small-scale circuits, called microcircuits, are found inside electrical devices, such as telephones, televisions, and radios.

MACROCIRCUITS

Electricity is generated in power stations (see pages 38–39). It leaves the power stations with a voltage of up to 400,000 volts and enters a grid—a network of wires and cables that spreads vast distances to carry electricity to wherever it is needed. The wires that carry the electricity are called transmission lines and are held high above the ground by pylons, or transmission towers.

In urban areas, transmission lines are buried beneath the ground. Substations reduce the voltage of electricity from 400,000 volts to 120 volts before it feeds into those circuits that supply streets and homes—mesocircuits.

▼ This photo of the world was taken from space. The light areas show where there is a large amount of electrical lighting in towns and cities.

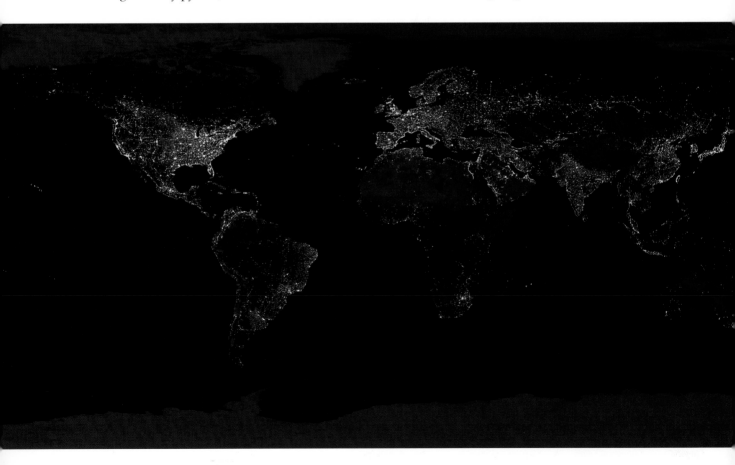

Mesocircuits to microcircuits

A household electric circuit carries electricity to all of the electric outlets in a house. By using switches, different parts of the circuit can be switched either on or off. When you use an electrical appliance, such as an electric heater or an alarm clock, the voltage in the electricity supply of the house forces electric current through the appliance.

Within the electric appliance there is another electric circuit, a microcircuit. The microcircuit uses electricity from the household supply to do its job, for example powering an alarm clock or stereo.

Microchips

Microchips are probably the most important invention of the last 500 years. They are found inside almost every modern electrical appliance, including televisions, DVD players, cars, and cell phones. Microchips are made from silicon, which is the main ingredient of beach sand. In laboratories, pure silicon rods are produced and then cut into thin wafers, much like very thin slices of cucumber. Electric microcircuits can be transferred onto the silicon wafers to create microchips. More than 100 microchips can be made from one silicon wafer. The microcircuits on the microchip include components such as

▲ Microcircuits similar to this one are found within most modern devices. The central black square is a microchip, which itself contains tiny microcircuits.

transistors (tiny electric switches) and light sources, just as in any electric circuit. More than 1,000 tiny switches could fit on the cross section of just one human hair, which itself is hard to see with the naked eye. You would not realize it, but there could be 10 million transistors in your home.

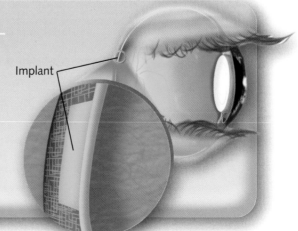

Did you know?

▶ Scientists have found a way to use silicon microchip technology to restore sight to the visually impaired. Patients with an eye disease called retinitis pigmentosa cannot see well at night and can only see straight ahead, as though they are looking through a tunnel. Scientists have implanted silicon chips a tenth of an inch (3 mm) long into the back of the eyes of such patients. The silicon chips change light into electrical signals, which the brain translates as images. Although still at an experimental stage, the results so far are better than expected, and all of the trial patients have reported improved sight.

Implant

Nanotechnology marks the beginning of a new age in science. The term "nanotechnology" comes from "nanometer." One nanometer is 0.00000004 inches, which is the equivalent of a line of 10 atoms. Nanotechnology refers to structures and machinery built on this scale, which have the potential to revolutionize our world and have an impact on almost every aspect of our lives. Some believe that nanotechnology could eliminate all common diseases, extend human capabilities, clean our environment, and generate cheap, pollution-free electricity.

Nanocomputers

Today's technology is clumsy. We move massive groups of atoms to create structures and machines. This has been likened to building a structure with small plastic bricks while wearing boxing gloves. Nanotechnology is like taking the boxing gloves off and manipulating individual atoms to create structures or machines from scratch.

Scientists are learning to use this "bottom-up" approach to build transistors (electric switches)

▼ **This is an actual photograph of a nanowire taken by a scanning tunneling micrograph. The wire is just 10 atoms wide.**

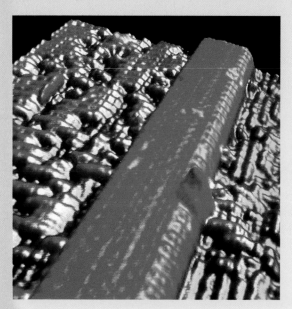

one atom at a time. Every particle in a microchip created in this way would have a purpose. Nanowires just one atom thick would form pathways in a circuit. Using nanoscale components, a computer the size of a human cell (around 15,000 nanometers) would have the same processing power as an entire human brain.

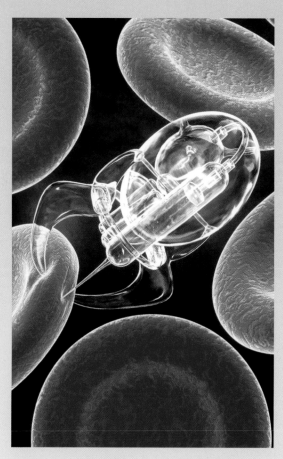

▲ **Nanobots in the bloodstream could target individual cells and inject them with medication.**

Nanobots and medicine

Human diseases and illnesses are often caused by damage inside our cells. Today's tools can be too big to tackle these problems. Nanobots (nanoscale robots) could be injected into the human body to scrub our veins and arteries clean of cholesterol, repair DNA, or inject medicines directly into our cells. We may even be able to create artificial cells to enhance human ability. An exploratory design of an artificial red blood cell suggests that such a cell could carry 236 times more oxygen than a living red blood cell. With this kind of capability, we would be able to hold our breath for 4 hours or sprint for 15 minutes without breathing at all.

Cleaning our world

Nanotechnology may also provide us with pollution-free electricity. By incorporating nanoscale solar cells into paint for road markings, we could generate masses of pollution-free electricity. Your house could be painted with a similar paint, and the electricity could be channeled directly to electric outlets.

Nanotechnology could help us clean up toxic chemical spills. Fleets of nanobots could rearrange the atoms of toxic substances into harmless chemicals. Nanomachines that look like microscopic trees could be used to soak up toxic chemicals from the ground. Their "leaves" would contain solar cells and provide the nanobot with energy; the roots would enter the ground and spread out to soak up toxic chemicals.

Our planet's ozone layer has been damaged by the release of chlorine-based chemicals into the atmosphere. To repair this, armies of nanoballoons could be programmed to collect the chlorine and combine it with sodium to create simple grains of salt, which would fall harmlessly back to Earth.

A nanotechnology gap?

In the same way that there is a technology gap between the **developed world** and the **developing world**, will there be a nanotechnology gap? Concerns include how and who should regulate it and who will own it. Will nanosensors invade privacy, and what is the likelihood of new toxic nanomaterials being created? There are currently no answers to these questions, but it is likely that nanotechnology will be with us, in one form or another, during our lifetimes.

▼ **Toxic chemical spills such as this one off the coast of Brazil could be tackled by nanobots.**

5

Magnets and magnetism

Magnetism is a basic force of nature. It controls the movement of electrons to generate electricity; it influences anything containing the metals iron, steel, nickel, or cobalt; it is a vital part of most machinery; and it helps migrating animals find their way. The biggest magnet on Earth is Earth itself. The smallest magnets are smaller than a pinhead. Both the natural magnets that form in Earth's crust and the strong, powerful magnets made by man act in a similar way. Here we look at magnets and magnetism to understand how they work.

MAGNETISM AND MAGNETIC FIELDS

One of the world's highest and fastest thrill rides, "Top Thrill Dragster" in Ohio, uses the force of magnetism. The ride rockets uphill, twists, and then drops 420 feet (128 m) at nearly 125 miles (200 km) per hour. The free-fall drop safely comes to a stop thanks to magnetic attraction between the train and the tracks.

Magnetism is a force that attracts and repels. Magnets are surrounded by a **magnetic field**, which is outlined by magnetic field lines. The field exists where the force of magnetism is strongest, and outside the field, the force fades away. All magnets have a north-seeking, or north, pole and a south-seeking, or south, pole. The magnetic field lines connect the poles because the opposite poles attract one another. The same poles of a magnet repel one another.

▼ Notice that the magnetic field lines never cross over each other. The lines spread out as they move away from the magnet, and the magnetic field weakens.

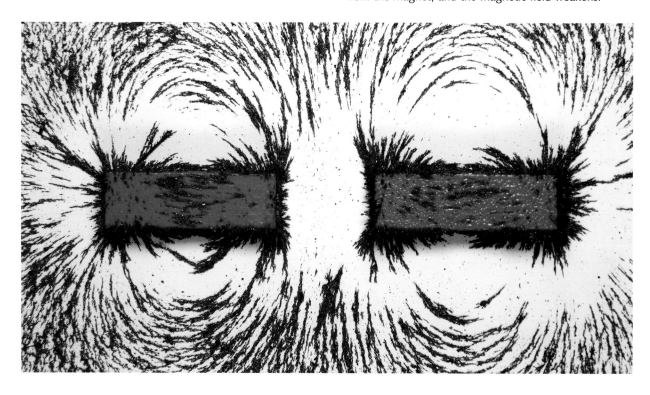

▶ Place a bar magnet on a white piece of paper. Sprinkle iron filings around it, and then tap the paper. The filings should arrange themselves into patterns of lines curving from one end of the magnet to the other, representing the magnetic field of the magnet. Try this experiment again with a horseshoe magnet. The iron filings should form a straight line between the two poles.

PLANET EARTH'S MAGNETISM

Earth acts like a giant magnet and has a magnetic north and south pole. These are not the same as the geographical North and South Poles, but they are nearby. It is believed that Earth's magnetic field is partly due to the high levels of iron in its core.

One of the oldest uses of Earth's magnetic field is in navigation. Compasses have helped travelers find their way for hundreds of years. Typical compasses have a magnetic needle balanced on the tip of a pin, which always points to Earth's magnetic north pole. Earth's magnetic field is curved, and the compass needle follows this curve. The needle is horizontal at the equator, but moving away from the equator in either direction causes the needle to tilt.

▶ In the northern hemisphere, the needle tilts downward to the north, while in the southern hemisphere the needle tilts downward to the south.

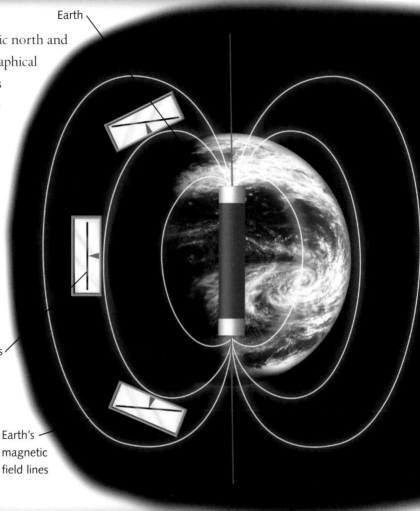

Earth

Compass

Earth's magnetic field lines

▶ Steel isn't always magnetic, but it is possible to magnetize a steel needle. Move a magnet in the same direction along the length of a steel needle. Do this at least 50 times.

This action causes the atoms in the needle to align and all point in the same direction, which is what makes the needle become magnetic.

To test whether the needle has become magnetized, hold it near a paper clip and see whether it is attracted.

Suspend the needle by a piece of cotton. The needle will react to Earth's magnetic field by aligning to the poles. As with any magnet, the needle will point to Earth's magnetic north pole.

VOLCANOES AND MAGNETS

Earth's solid inner core is surrounded by a molten, iron-rich layer, which can escape up through Earth's crust to the surface (a volcanic eruption). When it cools and hardens, it forms boulders that are naturally magnetic. If large magnetic boulders are broken down into smaller pieces, all of them become individual magnets. These are permanent magnets—they are always magnetic.

Magnetite, also called magnet stone or lodestone, is the most common natural permanent magnet. Chemically, it is called iron oxide, and it has a gray-black appearance. It is found in some rocks that make up Earth's surface. In those places, a compass would lead you around in circles because it would be influenced by the magnetite in the ground. Pyrrhotite, an iron sulfide, is the second most common natural permanent magnet. Its magnetism is so weak that it is detectable only when it is a powder, when it will coat a piece of iron with its dust.

▲ Volcanic eruptions spew molten lava, which can harden to form magnetic rocks.

DID YOU KNOW?

▶ At the University of Nijmegen in the Netherlands, scientists have levitated (floated) a live frog in midair. Strong magnets, around 1,000 times stronger than household magnets, repel the atoms of the frog's body. In theory, a powerful enough magnet would levitate a human freely in midair. In Japan, a mega-magnet was used to levitate a 300-pound (136 km) Sumo wrestler standing on an aluminium disc.

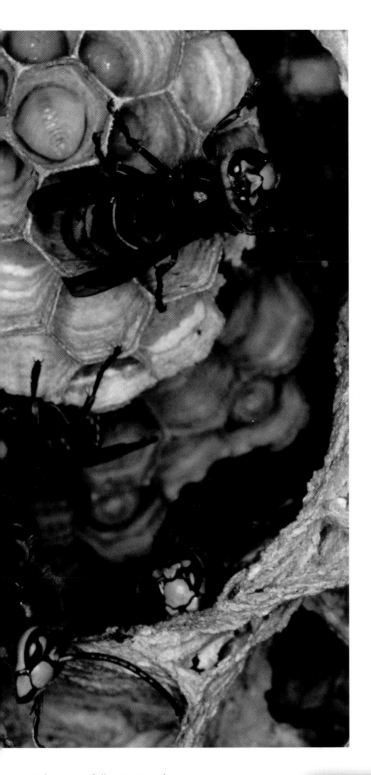

▲ These carefully structured and symmetrical cells are created by hornets with the help of tiny magnetic crystals.

MAGNETS AND LIVING CREATURES

In nature, some microscopic bacteria produce tiny particles of magnetite to help position themselves in relation to Earth's magnetic field. Scientists believe that they do this to migrate and find new food sources, instead of spinning around aimlessly. Hornets, a type of large wasp, also use magnets. Tiny crystals of a weakly magnetic material called ilmenite have been found in each of the cells of a hornets' nest. The ilmenite helps the hornets build symmetrical and uniform nests, in the same way that surveyors use tools to mark out the foundations for a building.

USEFUL MAGNETISM

Alloys (mixtures) of iron, nickel, and cobalt are manufactured into permanent magnets for use in some surprising places, such as vending machines and microphones. When you put coins in a vending machine to buy a bar of chocolate, a magnet checks that the money is genuine. Fake coins are generally more dense than genuine coins. The magnet checks the density and rejects the fakes. Microphones used for school assemblies and outdoor concerts also contain permanent magnets. When you speak into a microphone, the magnet moves, which produces an electric current in a wire. The current is amplified (made bigger) and directed through speakers to make it louder.

The phenomenon of magnetism has been known to humans for thousands of years. According to legend, Magnes, a shepherd in ancient Greece, noticed magnet stone when the iron-tipped end of his crook was pulled down toward certain rocks. The name "magnet stone" comes from the Greek "magnes lithos," which translates as "the stone of Magnes." Around 550 B.C., Thales, an ancient Greek philosopher, noticed that iron-containing magnet stones attracted iron and other magnet stones, and concluded that magnet stones must have a "soul." Many of the great ancient civilizations used magnetism for therapeutic purposes. One well-known story tells us that in ancient Egypt (c. 50 B.C.), Cleopatra adorned herself with magnetic jewelry and wore a magnetic stone on her forehead to preserve her youthfulness. Other civilizations, such as the Indians, Arabs, and Hebrews, also used magnetic stones for healing purposes.

▶ This is an early Chinese compass.

Early compasses

The Chinese were the first to use the properties of magnet stones to point out directions. From around A.D. 100, Chinese texts tell us of a "south pointer," which was used to decide the best location for burials and other rituals. These early compasses consisted of a square slab, representing Earth, and a bronze disc, representing heaven. Twenty-four directions were marked on the compass based on the position of stars in the night sky. The compass needle in the center of the disc was a spoon-shaped magnet stone with a handle that always pointed south.

Magnets and travel

Five hundred years later (c. A.D. 600), Chinese scholars discovered that they could magnetize iron needles by rubbing them with magnet stone. By A.D. 1000, they had devised ways to use the magnetized needle as a portable means of navigation. They floated the magnetized needles in water, suspended them from a silk thread, or placed them on a point. Tales of oriental magnetism spread, and by 1100, simple magnetic compasses were also in use in Europe, but little was known about how they worked.

experiments, one to show how a wire could be heated by an electric current, and the other to demonstrate magnetism. Instead, he made a groundbreaking discovery. He noticed that each time he switched on the electric current, the compass needle moved. This discovery and further research by Joseph Henry led to the invention of the electromagnet, which has dramatically changed our world (see pages 28–29). Today, magnetism is described by science as a basic force, because it exists without adequate explanation.

▲ A modern compass

Earth as a magnet

In English, the name for magnet stone became lodestone, because "lode" is an old word meaning "to guide the way." In 1492, Christopher Columbus sailed west from Spain, crossed the Atlantic, and discovered America. During his voyage, he noticed that the needle of his ship's compass had a tendency to tilt downward toward north. Other sailors also noticed this, but the first person to realize why was a British scientist named William Gilbert.

In 1600, he brilliantly and correctly suggested that Earth itself is a magnet and that the compass needle follows Earth's curved magnetic field. Having experimented with pieces of lodestone, he noticed that magnets have fields of force with what he called north and south poles. French scientist Rene Descartes experimented further with magnets and, in 1644, used iron filings to reveal the fields of force surrounding them for the first time.

Artificial magnets

In 1740, artificial magnets were produced for the first time and were sold to scientific investigators and navigators. For the next 60 years, magnets played little role in science. Then, in the early 1800s, Hans Oersted, a professor of science, arranged two

▲ Sailing ships have used compasses to guide them for centuries.

6

Electromagnetism

Electricity and magnetism are very closely linked. An electric current flowing through a wire has a force field similar to that of a magnet. If you hold a compass near an electrified wire, the needle swings away from its normal north-south position. If the electric current is switched off, the compass needle returns to its north-south position. Because a compass is affected only if an electric current is flowing through the wire, we can conclude that the electric current is generating an electromagnetic field.

HOW DO ELECTROMAGNETIC FIELDS WORK?

Electric currents cause atoms to behave in the same way as they do in a magnet. Steel becomes magnetized when its atoms line up and point in the same direction (see page 23). Each atom is like a tiny magnet, and when they join forces by pointing in one direction, the steel becomes magnetic. A copper wire itself isn't magnetic, but it is a good conductor of electricity. An electric current makes the copper atoms behave like lots of tiny magnets, or **electromagnets**. The copper atoms line up and generate a weak electromagnetic field.

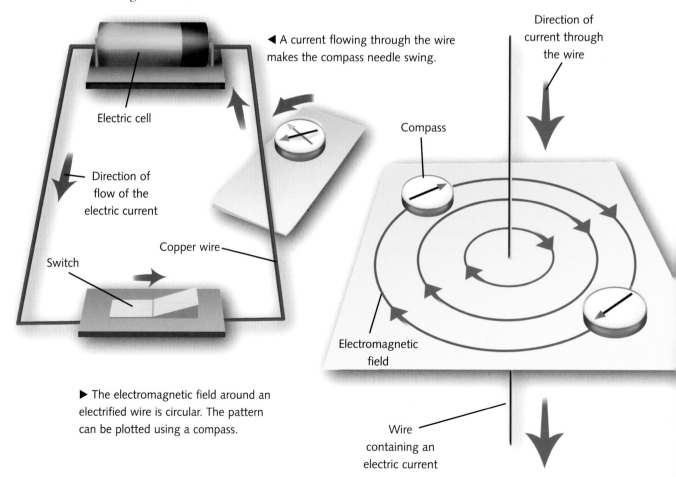

◄ A current flowing through the wire makes the compass needle swing.

Electric cell

Direction of flow of the electric current

Switch

Copper wire

Direction of current through the wire

Compass

Electromagnetic field

Wire containing an electric current

▶ The electromagnetic field around an electrified wire is circular. The pattern can be plotted using a compass.

SOLENOIDS AND ELECTROMAGNETS

A coiled wire with an electric current flowing through it creates a much stronger electromagnetic field than a straight wire. This is called a **solenoid**. The electromagnetic field pattern looks just the same as that of a bar magnet. The electromagnetic field can be made stronger by increasing the electric current, by making more turns in the coil, or by placing a rod of iron through the coil. If the iron rod is swapped for a steel rod, the electromagnetic field is less strong, and it remains magnetized after the current is switched off. This is undesirable because one of the most important properties of an electromagnet is that it can be switched on and off as required.

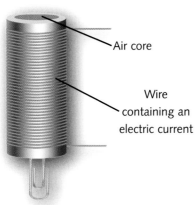

Air core

Wire containing an electric current

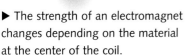

▶ The strength of an electromagnet changes depending on the material at the center of the coil.

Steel core

Iron core

TIME TRAVEL: DISCOVERIES OF THE PAST

In 1829, an American scientist, Joseph Henry, constructed the first electromagnet. It was an impressive device, capable of lifting a ton (1 t) of iron. Henry had discovered that the magnetic force is greatly increased by coiling the wire around an iron core. This multiplies the number of times the electric current passes in the same direction (as long as the current cannot jump from one loop to the next), which increases the strength of the magnetic field.

Henry's work helped to bring about the invention of the electric motor and the dynamo (generator). Most of the electricity we use today is produced by large dynamos that use powerful electromagnets.

▶ **Some cranes use strong electromagnets. Magnetic material is picked up when the current is on. The load is dropped when the electricity is stopped.**

LIVING WITH ELECTROMAGNETISM

Electromagnets are essential components of many modern devices, from electric motors in dishwashers, CD players, and car windshield wipers, to speakers in telephones and televisions. One of the most useful properties of electromagnets is that they can be switched on and off as required by turning off the electricity supply—something it is not possible to do with permanent magnets. Electric doorbells are a good example of the use of this property.

HOW AN ELECTRIC DOORBELL WORKS:

(1) The doorbell is pressed, which completes an electric circuit. An electric current flows around the circuit.

(2) The current flows through a wire wrapped around a soft iron core, which magnetizes it to create an electromagnet.

(3) The electromagnet attracts an iron hammer, or armature, which hits a bell.

(4) As the hammer hits the bell, it pulls the contacts apart, which breaks the circuit.

(5) With the circuit broken, the electric current stops flowing and the electromagnet loses its magnetism. The hammer moves back to its original position.

(6) This movement reconnects the circuit, and the cycle begins all over again. The bell is hit repeatedly while the doorbell is pressed.

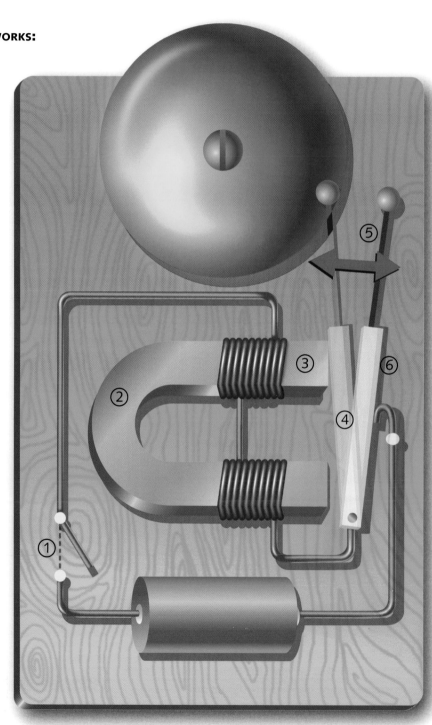

FLOATING TRAINS

In January 2004, after 70 years of maglev (magnetic levitation) technology development, the world's first commercially operated maglev train, the Shanghai Transrapid, entered service in Shanghai, China. It runs 18.5 miles (30 km) between Pudong International Airport and Shanghai's city center and is the fastest land-based transportation system in the world. It takes just two minutes to reach 186 miles (300 km) per hour, and its top speed is 268 miles (431 km) per hour.

Maglev trains levitate (hover) above their guideway using electromagnets. Instead of an engine, electromagnetic fields propel the train along and help it stop again. The speed is adjusted by changing the electric current. In test runs, maglev trains have reached incredible speeds of up to 310 miles (500 km) per hour. That's more than twice as fast as the fastest commuter train found in either the United States or the United Kingdom (UK). These speeds are achieved because the train moves along an entirely smooth surface—air. Maglev trains and their guideways are expensive to build and maintain, but there are plans for future developments in Germany, the Netherlands, and the U.S.

▼ Traveling on the Shanghai Transrapid is said to feel like flying.

ELECTROMAGNETISM IN HOSPITALS

Surgeons use electromagnets for removing fragments of iron or steel that have penetrated people's bodies—such as shrapnel from bomb blasts. This is much more hygienic and less painful than using tweezers. Strong electromagnets are also used in body scanners called magnetic resonance imaging (MRI) scanners. They align the billions of atoms in the body, and the scanner can then "read" which type of tissue is which. This safely forms an extraordinarily detailed 3D image of the inside of the human body, which is used in diagnosing and treating many illnesses.

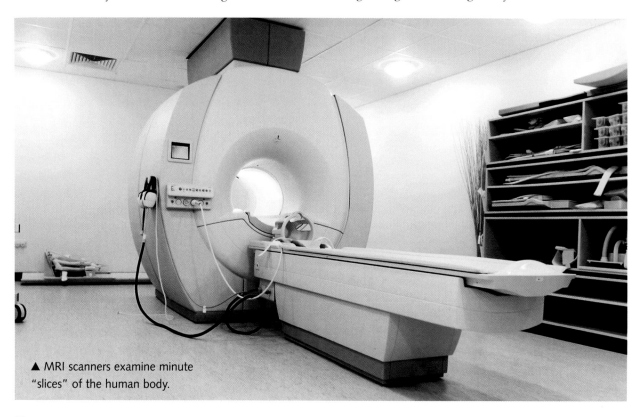

▲ MRI scanners examine minute "slices" of the human body.

ELECTROMAGNETISM HELPS HAIR GROWTH

Surprisingly, low-strength electromagnetic fields can help prevent hair loss in patients who are receiving chemotherapy. In a recent trial, patients sat under a device, which looks like a hair dryer, for brief periods of time during their 24-week treatment for breast cancer. Coils of wire inside the "hair dryer" created an electromagnetic field. All but one of the women kept their hair. It is thought that the electromagnetic field stimulates a hair growth hormone (chemical in the body).

DID YOU KNOW?

▶ The electromagnet in an MRI scanner is so strong that if you were to hold a steel wrench and stand three feet (0.9 m) away from the scanner, the wrench would be ripped from your grasp. Not surprisingly, iron and steel objects are banned in the scanning room.

TEST YOURSELF

▶ Name three ways in which an electromagnetic field can be made stronger.

▶ Give two reasons why electromagnets are more useful than permanent magnets in everyday life.

Electromagnetism in nature

Although the electromagnets found in modern devices are a human invention, electromagnetism also exists in the natural world. Earth's magnetic field is actually thought to be an electromagnetic field caused not only by Earth's iron-rich inner core, but also by the movement of a molten layer surrounding it. Scientists think that the molten layer, containing iron and nickel, acts in a similar way to the current flowing through a wire in an electromagnet. It travels around the inner core and generates an electromagnetic field.

STUNNING LIGHT DISPLAYS

Storms on the sun generate blasts of electrons and powerful winds that shock Earth's atmosphere. Earth's electromagnetic field repels most of this, but some leaks down to the atmosphere at the magnetic poles. As the electrons hit nitrogen and oxygen gas in the atmosphere, they emit beautiful displays of colored light, called the northern lights (aurora borealis) or southern lights (aurora australis). The exact colors in the display depend on which gas is hit. When oxygen atoms are hit, the light displays are green or red. When nitrogen is hit, the displays are blue, purple, or violet. People travel hundreds of miles to the extreme northern and southern parts of the globe to see these stunning displays.

▶ This is the aurora borealis over Alaska.

ANIMAL MAGNETISM

Each winter, migrating birds travel thousands of miles to reach warmer lands. Iron-based particles in their brains are influenced by Earth's electromagnetic field and tell the birds which direction they are heading. Hatching loggerhead turtles are able to navigate vast distances to safer waters by similar means. It is thought that all migratory animals—mammals, birds, reptiles, amphibians, fish, and invertebrates—use similar built-in mechanisms.

Sharks are highly effective predators and rely on their acute senses of smell, hearing, and taste to catch their prey. In addition to this, sharks have an extra sense. Sensors, called ampullae of Lorenzini, are located beneath the skin on their heads and allow them to detect electromagnetic signals coming from the muscles of their prey. These, combined with their other well-developed senses, make them formidable hunters.

▼ Sharks detect weak electromagnetic fields up to three feet (0.9 m) away—handy for detecting fish hiding on the seabed.

TIME TRAVEL: INTO THE FUTURE

Earth's core is always moving, and every 100,000 years or so, this movement results in the core flipping over. Earth's electromagnetic poles reverse—north becomes south, and south becomes north. Scientists know that this has happened because the evidence is left behind in hardened lava from volcanoes. Iron atoms in the lava point in a north-south direction, mirroring Earth's electromagnetic field at the moment at which it hardened. If this direction is different than today's electromagnetic field, we know that the poles have moved.

Earth's electromagnetic field has been weakening for the last 2,000 years. Although this could just be a natural variation, it may mean that we are due for a reversal in the next 1,000 to 2,000 years. The weakening has already resulted in malfunctions in some satellites that orbit Earth. Reversals can take 10,000 years to complete, and during this time Earth could have multiple poles.

Glitches in electrical equipment would become more common, and compasses would be useless, making navigation very confusing. Light displays—auroras—would increase as the electrons from the sun were drawn to the multiple poles of Earth. Fortunately, a slow reversal would give animals that use Earth's electromagnetic field for navigation time to reorientate themselves, and while a reversal is a certainty, it may not happen for millions of years.

The electromagnetic spectrum

Electromagnetic signals are a part of everyday life. They bring the pictures and sound to televisions, and they cook food in microwaves and enable communication through cell phones. Electromagnetic signals travel through air and can also travel through a vacuum (space containing nothing at all). Not all communication signals are electromagnetic. Plenty of devices send and receive electric signals along electric wires and cables; these signals are simply changes in the electric current.

THE ELECTROMAGNETIC SPECTRUM

Electromagnetic signals travel in waves, similar to waves rolling along in the ocean. Television signals, radio waves, light, microwaves, x-rays, cell phone signals, infrared radiation, and ultraviolet (UV) light are all electromagnetic waves. They are part of the **electromagnetic spectrum**.

Gamma rays—These powerful rays are given off by radioactive materials such as uranium, a heavy metal.

Ultraviolet light—This type of radiation is emitted by the sun and can burn human skin and cause skin cancer.

Infrared radiation—We feel this type of radiation as warmth. It is produced by the sun, radiators, and the human body.

Radio waves—These waves are emitted by radio and television stations. Stars also give off radio waves.

X-rays—This high-energy form of radiation can travel through skin and muscle but is stopped by bone.

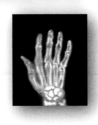

Visible light—Visible light waves are the only electromagnetic waves that humans can see with the naked eye.

Microwaves—This radiation heats objects through which it passes. Cell phone communication relies on microwaves.

HOW DOES TELEVISION WORK?

In many parts of the world, watching television is an extremely popular pastime. The average American will spend a total of 9 years watching television if he or she lives 65 years. But how does television work?

Televisions use a combination of electromagnetic and electric signals. Television programs are transmitted from the station as electromagnetic waves. The waves carry all of the information about the program—the pictures, the sound, and which channel it will go on. Relay stations receive the waves and send them on to television antennas.

▲ Television antennas like these collect electromagnetic signals. As satellite and cable television become more popular, these antennas are likely to disappear from use.

The antennas collect the electromagnetic waves and send them to the television along a wire or cable as electric signals.

Satellite television broadcasting works in a slightly different way—the information is sent as a digital signal. Digital signals travel better than electromagnetic waves. Man-made satellites orbiting Earth act as the relay station so that obstacles such as mountains are avoided. They collect and transmit the signal to satellite receivers. The signal travels along cables from the receiver to a decoder box and then to the television set. Cable television broadcasting sends digital signals along underground cables instead of to a satellite.

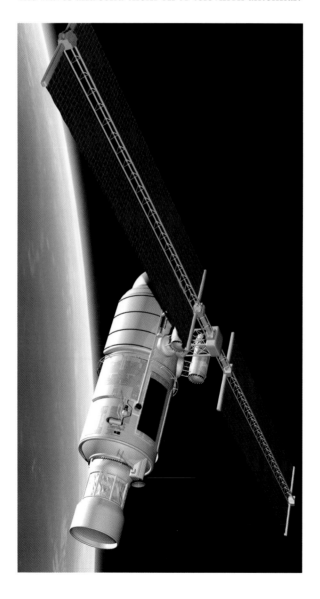

◀ Communication satellites act as relay stations. They transmit satellite television to homes.

INSIDE A TELEVISION

The majority of televisions rely on cathode ray tubes to project the electric signal from the antenna, satellite receiver, or cable onto the screen. "Cathode" is another name for a negative terminal, as in a battery. In a television, the cathode produces a stream of electrons, which travel at high speed through the cathode ray tube.

At the other end of the tube, the electrons strike a screen coated with phosphor, causing it to glow. An electromagnetic field guides the stream of electrons to hit the screen in the right places to produce up to 30 pictures a second. We don't see these as separate images; instead it looks to us like one continuous motion picture.

◄ Televisions rely on a combination of electric and electromagnetic signals. If you look closely at a television screen, you may be able to see separate dots of color. Your brain merges these together to form an image.

DID YOU KNOW?

▶ Humans glow in the dark. If you could see infrared radiation (heat), you would notice that warm-blooded animals constantly give out electromagnetic radiation. In this image, the red and orange indicate hotter areas, and blue and green represent colder areas. Not much infrared radiation is escaping through the baby's diaper. This photo was taken using a camera that detects infrared radiation, rather than visible light. Night vision goggles also detect infrared radiation. The police use night vision goggles to catch criminals at night. This is especially useful if the police are tracking a suspect from a helicopter. They can see the suspect even if he or she tries to hide in woods or bushes.

FLAT SCREENS

Flat screens, such as those on laptop computers, digital cameras, and cell phones, are grids of tiny cells containing a crystal-like substance. They are called liquid crystal displays (LCDs). Cell phones receive radio waves, a form of electromagnetic radiation, which they convert into an electric signal. The electric signal causes tiny particles of the liquid crystal to twist, so that they reflect (give off) light to create the words and pictures on the screen of the phone.

9

Energy and electricity

The electricity that we get out of outlets in our homes is produced by generators inside power stations. Generators contain a magnet and a loop of wire. Turbines rotate the loop of wire inside the magnetic field, and this causes electrons in the wire to flow. Where possible, power stations are built near their source of energy—their fuel. The majority of power stations burn **fossil fuels**, such as coal, oil, and gas. Electricity is a convenient form of energy because it is easily transported along cables and wires from power stations to wherever it is needed.

INSIDE A POWER STATION

A power station's fuel is burned in a furnace and produces heat. The heat is used to boil water and turn it into steam. Jets of this scalding steam travel down pipes to a turbine, which is similar to a large water wheel, but instead of being driven by water, it is driven by steam. The turbine is attached to a generator, and as it turns, it twists the loop of wire in the generator to produce electricity.

Nuclear power stations work in much the same way. Nuclear reactions produce heat, which is used to boil water and create steam to drive turbines and a generator. Electricity generated by all power stations enters circuits spanning hundreds of miles (see pages 18–19). From there, it travels to factories, homes, offices, schools, and many other areas of everyday life.

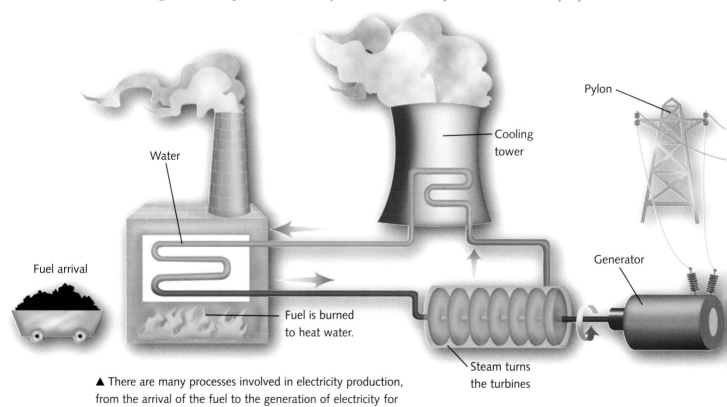

Pylon

Cooling tower

Water

Fuel arrival

Generator

Fuel is burned to heat water.

Steam turns the turbines

▲ There are many processes involved in electricity production, from the arrival of the fuel to the generation of electricity for use in your home.

▶ If you were to stand underneath an electricity pylon holding a fluorescent light bulb, it would glow. It works because the air surrounding the pylon is electrically charged. In 2004, a British sculptor used this effect to create a piece of artwork using lighting tubes near Bath, Britain.

▼ The wide chimneys release waste heat into the atmosphere. The thin chimneys release smoke.

POWER STATION CHIMNEYS

Huge power station chimneys appear to belt out smoke, but they actually release steam into the atmosphere. Once the steam has passed through the turbine, it is still very hot. It is cooled in a heat exchanger. During this process, the huge chimneys draw down air to ground level. This cools water in the heat exchanger, but some escapes into the atmosphere. This is the steam you see coming from the chimneys, or cooling towers.

TIME TRAVEL: INTO THE FUTURE

One of the biggest threats to our planet, and one that is likely to affect each of us in the future, is climate change. The burning of fossil fuels to produce electricity releases harmful gases into the atmosphere. The most problematic gas is carbon dioxide. As a result of burning fossil fuels, levels of carbon dioxide in the atmosphere have risen steadily over the years. That is why governments are encouraging the planting of trees, which absorb carbon dioxide and produce oxygen instead.

Too much carbon dioxide in the atmosphere traps heat and, in so doing, warms our climate. At the current rate of warming, the polar ice caps will begin to melt, leading to a 24-inch (60 cm) increase in sea levels by the end of this century. Many low-lying areas of land will be threatened, including cities such as New York, Mumbai, and Tokyo. Sixteen percent of Bangladesh could be covered by water within 50 years if something isn't done about the rising carbon dioxide levels. All countries of the world need to reduce carbon dioxide emissions by conserving energy and adopting more environmentally friendly ways of producing electricity.

10

Electricity and the environment

Fossil fuels provide around 66 percent of the world's electricity and 95 percent of the world's total energy demands, including heating, transportation, and electricity generation. However, burning fossil fuels pollutes our planet by changing the climate and causing acid rain. Individuals, companies, and governments are looking for alternative ways of producing electricity. Water, wind, and solar energy could offer us environmentally friendly electricity production in the future.

NONRENEWABLE AND RENEWABLE

Fossil fuels won't last forever; they are **nonrenewable**. Oil supplies are likely to be gone within 40 years—within your lifetime. Natural gas could last another 70 years, and coal could last another 190 years. Each year, we use more fossil fuels than the previous year, and reserves could last even less time than we thought. Nuclear fuels, which are also nonrenewable, are likely to become too expensive to obtain, and the radioactive waste products are extremely difficult to get rid of safely.

Time and effort have been put into developing **renewable** and **sustainable** energy sources. Renewable and sustainable fuels are those that will never run out, such as water, wind, and sunlight, and those that run out but can be replaced, such as methane gas from manure or wood from trees.

HYDROELECTRIC POWER

Water is currently the most commonly used sustainable energy resource, providing enough power to meet the needs of 28.3 million consumers in the U.S. alone. Dams trap large volumes of water in man-made lakes, or reservoirs. The water is released through a turbine connected to a generator, which produces electricity. The problem with large dams is that their construction destroys

▲ Fifteen million gallons (57 million l) of water can pass through the Glen Canyon dam in the U.S. each minute to supply 1.5 million customers with electricity.

vast areas of natural habitat, villages, and towns, and they slowly fill up with silt, reducing the amount of water they can hold.

ELECTRICITY FROM TIDES

Water in other forms also contains a lot of energy. The energy of tides can be harnessed to produce electricity by building a structure similar to a dam, called a tidal barrage, in the sea or ocean. Tidal barrages trap water at high tide and let it out through turbines at low tide to generate electricity. Alternatively, underwater turbines can be built, which spin as the tide goes in and out. There are three tidal power plants in the world, the largest of which is La Rance, in France. Other sites have been suggested in the U.S., the UK, Norway, and South Korea.

ELECTRICITY FROM WAVES

Waves are caused by the wind blowing over the surface of the sea or ocean. Waves can be harnessed to generate electricity by focussing them into a narrow channel and using them to spin turbines. The west coasts of the U.S. and Europe and the coasts of Japan and New Zealand are good sites for harnessing wave energy. However, because waves are not a reliable form of energy, and the energy is difficult to harness, there are currently no commercial wave power plants. Further research is required before engineers make wave machines efficient enough.

▲ Some people think that wind farms spoil areas of natural beauty and harm wildlife.

ELECTRICITY FROM THE WIND

Wind is used to turn turbines and generate electricity. It is one of the fastest-growing sustainable energy technologies. In the U.S., wind power provides electricity for around two million homes. More recently, large offshore wind farms have been built where wind speeds are higher. The largest offshore wind farm in the world is at Horns Rev in Danish waters. It supplies 150,000 homes with electricity. By 2030, it is estimated that more than 25 percent of Denmark's electricity will be generated by offshore wind farms.

▶ Solar panels could be particularly useful in providing electricity for remote towns in developing countries.

ELECTRICITY FROM THE SUN

The sun is 93 million miles (150 million km) from us, and every minute, enough energy reaches Earth to power our world for a whole year. Solar panels turn sunlight into electricity. The panels have two layers of silicon. The arriving light causes electrons to travel from one silicon layer to the other, which generates an electric current. In the U.S., around 10,000 homes are powered entirely by solar power. As the panels become cheaper to manufacture, they will be found increasingly on homes, cars, and perhaps even clothing to power small electronic devices.

THE FUTURE

Electricity generation in the future is likely to rely on a combination of hydroelectric, tidal, wave, wind, and solar technologies. Other energy sources, such as the heat energy produced by Earth and the energy from waste products, are also likely to supply some electricity.

11

Relying on electricity

Today, most people in the developed world take electricity for granted. However, it isn't all that long since it was first introduced into our lives. In the middle of the 1800s, industry began using electricity, and over the second half of the century, electrical devices were enjoyed only by industry and the wealthy. Gradually, electricity became familiar in the form of lighting for streets, public buildings, offices, hotels, and restaurants, and for powering public transportation.

ACCEPTANCE OF ELECTRICITY

Before 1920, most people did not understand electricity very well and were worried about the dangers. However, as soon as safe switches and outlets and insulated wire were developed, increasing numbers of ordinary people embraced the electrical age. By the 1940s, new generations were growing up with electricity as something they took for granted. In the developed world, the whole infrastructure of civilization would grind to a halt without electricity. Almost every aspect of our lives involves electricity in one way or another.

ELECTRICITY BLACKOUT

In 2003, the U.S. and Canada were hit by one of the largest electricity blackouts in history. On August 14, a chain of events resulted in the shutdown of 100 power plants, leaving millions of people without electricity. There was no way of lighting homes, offices, and streets; cell phone networks jammed; and trains and planes could not operate. It was impossible to get gas from the electricity-powered pumps, and in high-tech buildings, toilets would not flush and faucets did not work, and in places where water was electrically pumped, there was no water at all. No one could get any cash from an ATM, and credit cards were useless. Fortunately, the 2003 blackout lasted less than a day, but it was a clear example of how electricity runs our lives.

◄ The New York City train and subway systems did not work during the 2003 blackout, and thousands of commuters had to walk home.

▶ How would you travel long distances, keep your food cool, cook your dinner, light your home, and entertain yourself without electricity?

WHY TREAT ELECTRICITY WITH RESPECT?

The human body conducts electricity. Severe electric shocks can cause burns both on the outside and the inside of the body. Electricity disrupts the body's functions and can cause death.

Electricity can travel through water. Touching wires or switches with wet hands can result in a serious electric shock. It is particularly dangerous to remain on a wet surface in a thunderstorm. People are killed every year by lightning strikes.

Electricity carried in overhead cables can jump between 14 and 16 inches (35–40 cm). Most overhead electricity cables are made of aluminum and are not insulated. Electricity will jump to any nearby object that will provide a route to the ground, including humans.

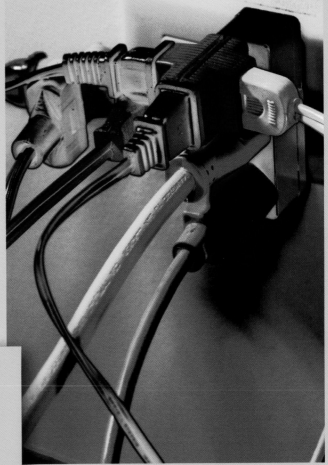

DANGER OF DEATH
KEEP OUT

Electricity can cause fire. The weight of the plugs and cables in an overloaded outlet (above) can pull them away from each other and cause heat and sparks.

Electricity can travel down kite strings or wires, which makes flying a kite or balloon near a power line very dangerous.

◀ Never ignore warning symbols such as this one. They are there to keep us safe.

Time travel: Electricity through the ages

Before 1550 B.C.—Prehistoric people witness electricity in the form of lightning and magnetism in the form of the iron ore "magnetite."

1550–146 B.C.—Ancient Greeks experiment with static electricity and magnetism.

A.D. 200–1100—The compass is developed in China, and its use spreads across the globe.

1492—Italian explorer Christopher Columbus uses a compass to navigate across the Atlantic Ocean from Spain to the "New World." He notices that the compass needle has a tendency to dip.

1600—British scientist William Gilbert suggests that Earth is a giant magnet. He describes repulsion and attraction in magnets and invents the concept of north and south poles.

▼ Our planet is a huge magnet.

1663—German scientist Otto Von Geuricke builds a machine for generating static electricity.

1683—British scientist Jean Theophile Desaguliers invents the terms "conductor" and "insulator."

1729—British scientist Stephen Gray becomes the first to demonstrate that static electricity can be made to flow along conducting wires.

1752—Scientist Benjamin Franklin shows that lightning is a form of static electricity by using the wet string of a kite to conduct lightning down from the sky.

1800—Italian scientist Alessandro Volta invents the first electric cell, or battery, known as the voltaic pile, which enables later scientists to experiment with current electricity.

1807—Danish scientist Hans Christian Oersted looks for a connection between current electricity and magnetism, having found that both electric currents and magnets possess similar fields of force.

1819—Oersted shows that a magnetized compass needle moves in the presence of an electric current.

1823—French scientist Andre-Marie Ampere establishes the relationship between electricity and magnetism.

1829—U.S. scientist Joseph Henry invents the electromagnet.

1831—Although working separately and in different countries, Joseph Henry and British scientist Michael Faraday build the first electric motor and electric generator.

1838—Michael Faraday discovers that electrified gases glow—the principle behind neon, sodium vapor, and mercury vapor lamps.

1845—Michael Faraday proposes that light is a form of electromagnetism.

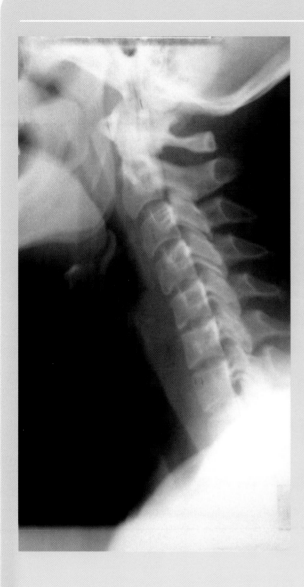

1900—German scientist Paul Karl Ludwig Drude demonstrates that an electric current is a flow of electrons.

1918–19—Electric washing machines and refrigerators first become available.

1930–40s—Hydroelectric power stations are built, but the majority of electricity is still generated from burning coal. Radios, vacuum cleaners, electric irons, and refrigerators become part of nearly every household.

1947—The transistor is invented.

1956—The world's first large-scale nuclear power station opens at Calder Hall in Cumbria, Britain.

1985—The world's first electricity-generating wind farm is built in California.

2000—The world's first wave power station is built on the Scottish island of Islay. Researchers are developing this model for commercial use in other parts of the world.

2005—Research into renewable technologies continues, but more than 90 percent of the world's electricity still comes from nonrenewable energy sources. Wind power (below) is one of the fastest-growing renewable energy technologies.

1873—British scientist James Clerk Maxwell reveals the basic laws of electromagnetism and predicts radio waves.

1888—German scientist Heinrich Hertz proves that electricity can be transmitted in electromagnetic waves. His experiments lead to the development of the radio.

1895—German scientist Wilhelm Konrad Roentgen discovers x-rays.

1897—British scientist Joseph John Thomson discovers the electron.

Glossary

CIRCUIT – A closed path along which an electric current can flow. Circuits include a power supply, such as a battery, conducting wires, and components, such as light bulbs and motors.

CONDUCTORS – Substances that allow an electric current to travel through them. Copper wire is a good conductor of electricity.

CURRENT ELECTRICITY – (see electric current)

DEVELOPED WORLD – Richer and more industrialized areas of the world, such as Australasia, North America, and western Europe.

DEVELOPING WORLD – Poorer and less industrialized areas of the world, such as large parts of Africa.

ELECTRIC CELL – A single unit that converts chemical energy into electrical energy. When two or more electric cells are joined together, the resulting unit is called a battery.

ELECTRIC CURRENT – A flow of electric charge. An ammeter is used to measure electric current in a circuit.

ELECTROMAGNETIC SPECTRUM – The entire range of radiation, which includes gamma rays, x-rays, ultraviolet radiation, visible light, infrared radiation, microwaves, and radio waves.

ELECTROMAGNETS – Coils of insulated wire, usually wrapped around a soft iron core, that are magnetized only when an electric current flows through the wire. Electromagnets are usually stronger than permanent magnets.

ELECTROSTATIC CHARGE – (see static electricity)

FOSSIL FUELS – Naturally occurring fuels, including coal, crude oil, and natural gas, which have formed over millions of years. They are burned in power stations to produce electricity.

FUSES – Safety devices that break a circuit when the electric current becomes too strong. This cuts off the flow of the electric current and can prevent overheating, which may otherwise cause a fire.

INSULATORS – Materials that prevent the flow of electric charge. Rubber is a good insulator.

ANSWERS

page 8 Investigate
The balloon sticks to the wall because you have rubbed electrons from the sweater onto the balloon. The electrons on the balloon repel the electrons on the wall, which makes the wall positively charged. Therefore, the balloon and the wall are attracted to each other, and the balloon sticks.

page 11 Investigate
If you can feel a slight tingle, then you have created a battery and a circuit. The tingle is the electricity traveling across your tongue.

page 17 Test yourself
Measuring electric current and voltage in series and parallel circuits can be seen on pages 15 and 16. In a series circuit, the ammeter can be placed anywhere to measure electric current. In a series circuit, the voltmeter should be placed across the component, such as the light bulb. In a parallel circuit, the ammeter will give different readings depending on how many parallel lines there are in the circuit. To measure the entire current, the ammeter should be placed either just before or just after the electricity supply—before the circuit splits. The voltmeter should be placed across a component, such as the light bulb.
All eleven electrical symbols:

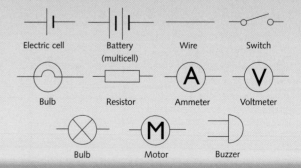

Electric cell   Battery (multicell)   Wire   Switch

Bulb   Resistor   Ammeter   Voltmeter

Bulb   Motor   Buzzer

46

MAGNETIC FIELD – An area over which a magnet can exert a magnetic force. A magnet's magnetic field can be viewed by sprinkling iron filings around the magnet. The filings will arrange themselves in lines that represent the magnetic field.

NONRENEWABLE – A resource that can be used only once and cannot be replaced. Although fossil fuels form underground constantly, they take millions of years to form. Therefore, they are considered to be nonrenewable.

POTENTIAL DIFFERENCE – This is another term for voltage (see voltage entry). It is a measure of the difference in voltage between two points in a circuit. A voltmeter is used to measure voltage in a circuit.

RENEWABLE – A resource that can be renewed naturally. Solar, wind, and water energy are all renewable resources, as they will continue to provide energy indefinitely.

RESISTANCE – The forced slowing down of electric current passing through a component in a circuit. The filament of a light bulb provides resistance in a circuit. The slower electric current heats the filament and causes it to glow white-hot.

SHORT CIRCUIT – An unwanted electrical connection that causes the electric current to bypass some of a circuit. Sparks from short circuits can cause fires.

SOLENOID – A cylindrical coil of insulated wire connected in a circuit. A solenoid is the basis of an electromagnet and has a magnetic field. Each coil increases the number of times the electricity passes in one direction. Therefore, the more coils present in a solenoid, the stronger the magnetic field.

STATIC ELECTRICITY – Charge that has accumulated on the surface of an object. Lightning is caused by static electricity. Static electricity builds up in clouds during a storm and eventually discharges by jumping from the cloud to the ground, or from one cloud to another.

SUSTAINABLE – A resource that is replenishable within a human lifetime and causes no long-term damage to the environment.

VOLTAGE – The force that pushes an electric current around a circuit. Small electric cells have low voltages—around 12 volts—but power lines into homes have a higher voltage—around 120 volts in the U.S. Voltage is another term for potential difference.

page 23 Investigate (top of page)
The lines made by your iron filings represent the magnetic lines of force of the magnets.

page 23 Investigate (bottom of page)
If you have caused the atoms of your needle to align, it will be magnetic and will point in the north-south direction when suspended. If it has not become magnetized, repeat the experiment, but this time draw the magnet in the same direction along the needle 100 times instead of 50 times.

page 25 Test yourself
The needle would not become magnetized because rubbing a needle back and forth with a magnet does not align all the atoms in the same direction. Instead, it pulls them first one way and then another.

page 32 Test yourself
An electromagnetic field can be made stronger by (1) making more turns in the wire, (2) placing a core of iron in the middle of the coil of wire, and (3) increasing the electric current running through the wire. Electromagnets are more useful than permanent magnets because (1) they are usually stronger than permanent magnets, and (2) the electromagnetism can be switched on and off as required.

page 43 Test yourself
Food could be kept cool underground or underwater. You would have to walk, bike, or travel by horseback to get anywhere. You would have to use a coal-, wood-, or gas-burning stove, or a grill to cook food. Lighting would have to come from candles, oil, or gas-powered lanterns, or from a fire. Entertainment could be playing board games, talking to your friends, or playing a sport such as football.

Index

Page references in italics represent pictures.

PHOTO CREDITS – **Cover background image** Rob Matheson/CORBIS **Front cover images** (l) www.istockphoto.com/ Thomas Mounsey (r) www.istockphoto.com/James McQuillan **Back cover image** (inset) www.istockphoto.com/Thomas Mounsey **p.1** (tr) Roger Tidman/CORBIS (bl) www.istockphoto.com/Thomas Mounsey (br) www.istockphoto.com/Scott Cressman **p.2** www.istockphoto.com/Jostein Hauge **p.3** (top) www.istockphoto.com/ BlaneyPhoto (b) www.istockphoto.com/José Carlos Pires Pereira **p.4** (tl) Stuart Westmorland/CORBIS (tr) Coneyl Jay/Science Photo Library (bl) www.istockphoto.com/ Mark Evans (br) Dr. Arthur Tucker/Science Photo Library **p.5** www.istockphoto.com/Mark Evans **p.6** Joseph Sohm; ChromoSohm Inc./CORBIS **p.7** www.istockphoto. com/BlaneyPhoto **p.8** Roger Ressmeyer/CORBIS **p.9** Rob Matheson/CORBIS **p.10** www.istockphoto.com/Mark Evans **p.11** Archivo Iconografico, S.A./CORBIS **p.12** Photodisc **p.14** Reuters/CORBIS **p.15** Reuters/CORBIS **p.17** (t) Science Photo Library (m) Jean-Loup Charmet/Science Photo Library (b) Bettmann/CORBIS **p.18** NASA's Earth Observatory, Craig Mayhew and Robert Simmon, NASA GSFC, based on DMSP data **p.19** www.istockphoto.com/ James McQuillan **p.20** (bl) Hewlett-Packard Laboratories/Science Photo Library **p.20** (tr) Coneyl Jay/Science Photo Library **p.21** Reuters/CORBIS **p.22** www.istockphoto.com/Thomas Mounsey **p.24** Bernhard Edmaier/Science Photo Library **p.24–25** Roger Tidman/CORBIS **p.26** Liu Liqun/CORBIS **p.27** (t) www.istockphoto.com/José Carlos Pires Pereira (b) Bettmann/CORBIS **p.29** Simon Fraser/Science Photo Library **p.31** Transrapid International GmbH & Co. KG **p.32** Gusto/Science Photo Library **p.33** Joshua Strang/U.S. Airforce/ZUMA/Corbis **p.34** Stuart Westmorland/CORBIS **p.36** (bl) www.istockphoto.com/Mark Evans (tr) Peter Barrett/CORBIS **p.37** (t) www.istockphoto.com/Matthias Weinrich (b) Dr. Arthur Tucker/Science Photo Library **p.39** (t) www.istockphoto.com/Joe Gough (b) Sanford/Agliolo/CORBIS **p.40** Buddy Mays/CORBIS **p.41** (t) Chinch Gryniewicz; Ecoscene/CORBIS (b) Owaki - Kulla/CORBIS **p.42** Reuters/CORBIS **p.43** (t) Denis Scott/CORBIS (b) www.istockphoto.com/Jostein Hauge **p.44** NASA **p.45** (t) www.istockphoto.com/Tomas Kraus (b) www.istockphoto.com/Scott Cressman